# Highlights

K

AGES 5-6

# Reading

## Learning Fun Workbook

For information about permission to reproduce selections from this book for
an entire school or school district, please contact permissions@highlights.com.

Published by Highlights Learning • 815 Church Street • Honesdale, Pennsylvania 18431
ISBN: 978-1-68437-286-7
Mfg. 04/2021
Printed in Madison, WI, USA
First edition
1 0 9 8 7 6 5

For assistance in the preparation of this book, the editors would like to thank:
Vanessa Maldonado, MSEd; MS Literacy Ed. K–12; Reading/LA Consultant Cert.; K–5 Literacy Instructional Coach
Kristin Ward, MS Curriculum, Instruction, and Assessment; K–5 Mathematics Instructional Coach
Jump Start Press, Inc.

# Alphabet Garden

Say each letter out loud as you follow the path.

Help Bari Bunny find her way through the garden maze. First, follow the uppercase letters in order from **A** to **Z**. Then cross the bridge and follow the lowercase letters from **a** to **z**.

# Aa

This is an uppercase A.

This is a lowercase a.

Trace and write uppercase **A** and lowercase **a**.

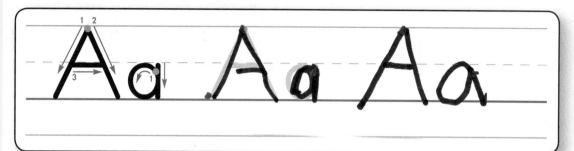

Now trace each **A** and **a** to finish the tongue twister. See if you can say it five times, fast!

Ashley is an astronaut.

How many **A**'s and **a**'s can you find in this picture?

**Short *a* makes the *ah* sound, as in *hat*. Long *a* makes the *ay* sound, as in *cake*.**

Read each word out loud. Draw a circle around each word that has the short **a** sound. Draw a rectangle around each word that has the long **a** sound.

tag

ant

apron

gate

cab

rake

# Bb

This is an uppercase B.

This is a lowercase b.

Now trace each **B** and **b** to finish the tongue twister. See if you can say it five times, fast!

Barney is a
baby bat.

These friends are building a statue. Write the letter **b** to complete the words. Draw a line from each word to the matching object in the picture.

____ird

____eaver

____ranch

# Cc

This is an uppercase C.

This is a lowercase c.

Trace and write uppercase C and lowercase c.

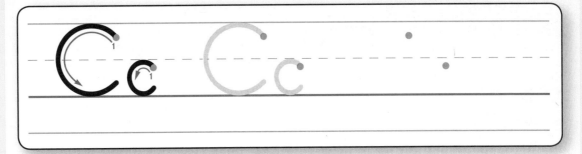

Now trace each C and c to finish the tongue twister. See if you can say it five times, fast!

Cora has a
cup of cocoa.

Draw a line between the 2 cupcakes that look the same. What could you do to make the other 2 cupcakes match each other?

# Dd

This is an uppercase D.

This is a lowercase d.

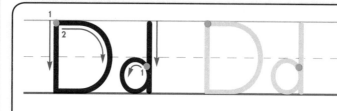

Now trace each **D** and **d** to finish the tongue twister. See if you can say it five times, fast!

David dived

down deep.

Look at these dinosaur doubles. Find and circle at least **5** differences.

# It's Rhyme Time!

Read the name of each object. Draw lines to match the names that rhyme.

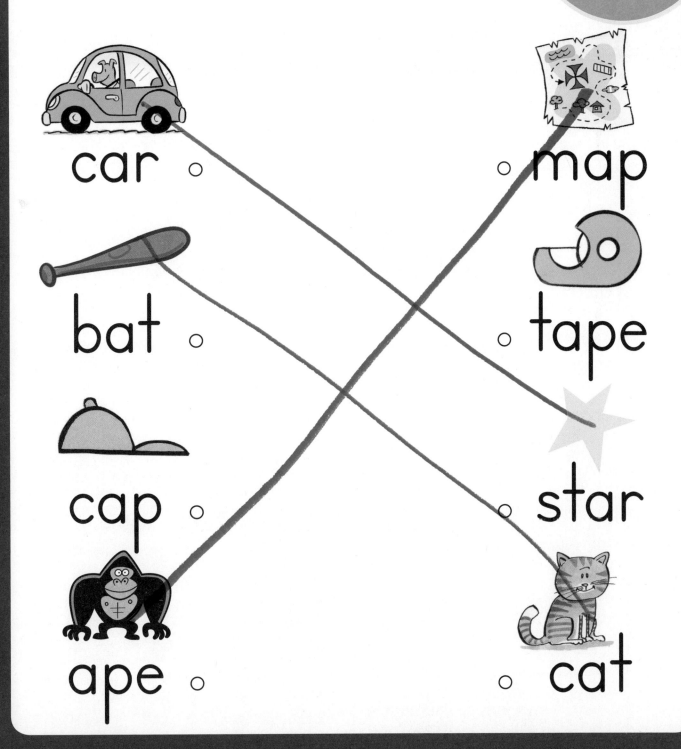

car

bat

cap

ape

map

tape

star

cat

# Ee

This is an uppercase **E**.

This is a lowercase **e**.

Trace and write uppercase **E** and lowercase **e**.

Now trace each **E** and **e** to finish the tongue twister. See if you can say it five times, fast!

Eli elephant exercises.

Can you find the **5** objects in this Hidden Pictures® puzzle?

cane

tennis ball

pear

magnet

necktie

Short *e* makes the *eh* sound, as in *beg*. Long *e* makes the *eey* sound, as in *tree*.

Read each word out loud. Draw a circle around each word that has the short **e** sound. Draw a rectangle around each word that has the long **e** sound.

nest

tree

3 three

bed

vet

bee

# Ff

This is an uppercase **F**.

This is a lowercase **f**.

Trace and write uppercase **F** and lowercase **f**.

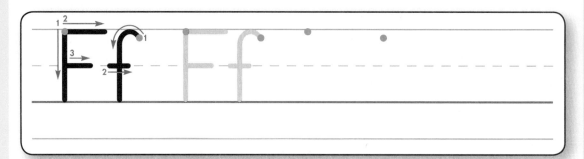

Now trace each **F** and **f** to finish the tongue twister. See if you can say it five times, fast!

Fifi is my furry friend.

How many **F**'s can you find at this Fourth of July picnic?

# Gg

This is an uppercase G.

This is a lowercase g.

What other words can you think of that start with the letter *g*?

Trace and write uppercase **G** and lowercase **g**.

Now trace each **G** and **g** to finish the tongue twister. See if you can say it five times, fast!

Gary the Goat

gets a grape.

Gabi is having a bowling birthday party. Write the letter **g** to complete the words. Use each word in an oral sentence about Gabi's party.

\_irl

\_ame

\_ifts

\_ood

# Hh

This is an uppercase H.

This is a lowercase h.

Trace and write uppercase **H** and lowercase **h**.

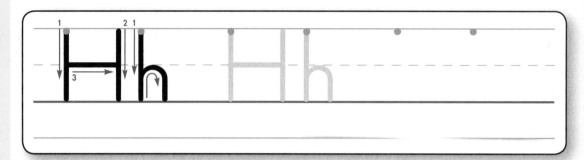

Now trace each **H** and **h** to finish the tongue twister. See if you can say it five times, fast!

Holly holds her hula hoop.

Which 2 horses are the same? Write an **H** on each matching horse.

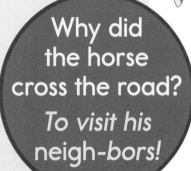
**Why did the horse cross the road?**
*To visit his neigh-bors!*

# It's Rhyme Time!

Look at the groups of objects. Read the name of each object out loud. Then cross out the object whose name does not rhyme with the others.

Which rhyming words have a short *e* sound? Which have a long *e* sound?

ten

hen

bell

pen

eel

tree

key

bee

# I i

This is an uppercase I.

This is a lowercase i.

Trace and write uppercase **I** and lowercase i.

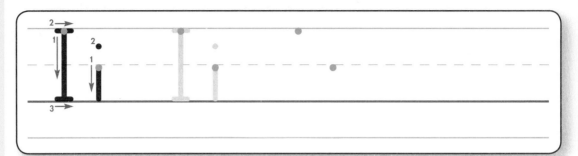

Now trace each **I** and **i** to finish the tongue twister. See if you can say it five times, fast!

Izzy glides
across the ice.

Can you find the **4** objects in this Hidden Pictures® puzzle?

**What do all these objects have in common?**

ivy leaf

iron

ice-cream cone

igloo

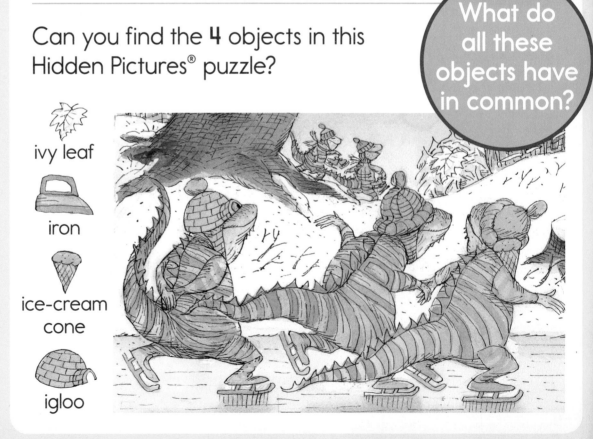

Short *i* makes the *ih* sound, as in *pin*. Long *i* makes the *eye* sound, as in *mine*.

Read each word out loud. Draw a circle around each word that has the short i sound. Draw a rectangle around each word that has the long i sound.

pig

ice cream

igloo

ring

hive

kite

# Jj

This is an uppercase J.

This is a lowercase j.

Trace and write uppercase **J** and lowercase **j**.

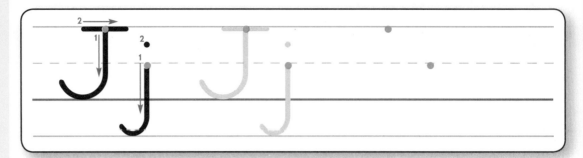

Now trace each **J** and **j** to finish the tongue twister. See if you can say it five times, fast!

Julie juggles joyfully.

Jack and Jane are exploring. How many **J**'s are in the jungle around them?

# Kk

This is an uppercase K.

This is a lowercase k.

Trace and write uppercase **K** and lowercase **k**.

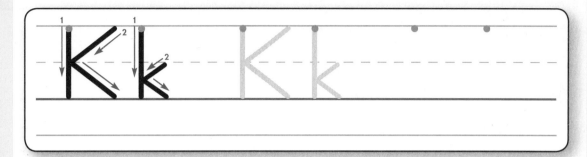

Now trace each **K** and **k** to finish the tongue twister. See if you can say it five times, fast!

Katie the

kangaroo kicks.

Read the **k** words. Draw a line from each key to the lock that has the same word.

# Ll

This is an uppercase L.

This is a lowercase l.

Trace and write uppercase **L** and lowercase **l**.

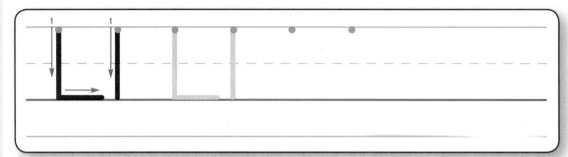

Now trace each **L** and **l** to finish the tongue twister. See if you can say it five times, fast!

## Lucy llama folds laundry.

Connect the dots from **A** to **L** to see what the lambs will use after their bath.

# Mm

This is an uppercase M.

This is a lowercase m.

What other words can you think of that start with the letter m?

Trace and write uppercase **M** and lowercase **m**.

Now trace each **M** and **m** to finish the tongue twister. See if you can say it five times, fast!

Mules melt marshmallows.

Write the letter **m** to complete the words. Then use each word in an oral sentence to tell about the picture.

__agic

__oose

__akes

__erry

# Nn

This is an uppercase N.

This is a lowercase n.

Trace and write uppercase **N** and lowercase **n**.

Now trace each **N** and **n** to finish the tongue twister. See if you can say it five times, fast!

Nicki saw a necklace in the nest.

Circle the things that start with the letter **n**.

net

nine

lamp

cow

dog

nurse

# Heard Word

These 8 pairs of rhyming words appear in the scene below. Draw a line from each word to its rhyming match. Then find and circle each pair in the picture.

fish ○                    ○ stripe

frog ○                    ○ hug

bug ○                     ○ jog

bear ○                    ○ mail

pipe ○                    ○ car

cat ○                     ○ dish

star ○                    ○ mat

snail ○                   ○ chair

**Can you find any other rhyming pairs in this picture?**

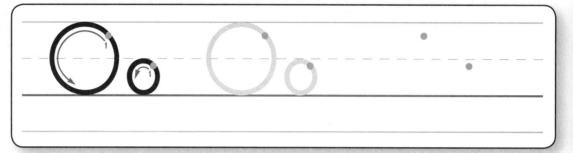

Oo

**This is an uppercase O.**

**This is a lowercase o.**

Trace and write uppercase O and lowercase o.

Now trace each O and o to finish the tongue twister. See if you can say it five times, fast!

# The owls are on an oak.

Olive the Octopus lives in the ocean. Draw a picture to show other animals that live in the ocean with her.

**Short o makes the *ahh* sound, as in *box*. Long o makes the *oh* sound, as in *home*.**

Read each word out loud. Draw a circle around each word that has the short o sound. Draw a rectangle around each word that has the long o sound.

oatmeal

mop

olive

bone

rocket

hole

# Pp

This is an uppercase P.

This is a lowercase p.

Trace and write uppercase **P** and lowercase **p**.

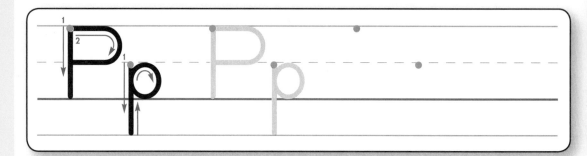

Now trace each **P** and **p** to finish the tongue twister. See if you can say it five times, fast!

Patrick picked a pickle.

Follow the **P**'s to help the penguin mom find her chick.

**Start**

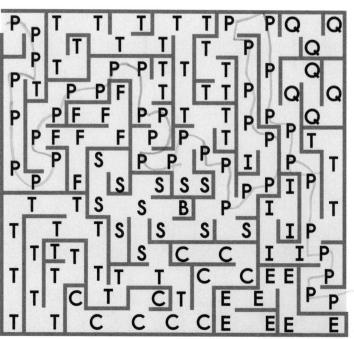

**Finish**

# Qq

This is an uppercase Q.

This is a lowercase q.

Now trace each **Q** and **q** to finish the tongue twister. See if you can say it five times, fast!

Quincy quizzed the queen.

Write **q** to complete the words. Read each word out loud. Then use crayons or markers to decorate the quilt.

__uiet

__uit

__uiz

__uarter

# Rr

This is an uppercase **R**.

This is a lowercase **r**.

Trace and write uppercase **R** and lowercase **r**.

Now trace each **R** and **r** to finish the tongue twister. See if you can say it five times, fast!

## Robbie rows the rowboat.

These **5** objects begin with the letter **r**. Can you find them in this Hidden Pictures® puzzle?

rake

rattle

ribbon

raspberry

roller skate

# Ss

This is an uppercase S.

This is a lowercase s.

What other words can you think of that start with the letter s?

Trace and write uppercase **S** and lowercase **s**.

Ss Ss

Now trace each **S** and **s** to finish the tongue twister. See if you can say it five times, fast!

Sadie spots a spider.

Each sock except **I** has an exact match. Can you find the sock with no match?

# Tt

This is an uppercase T.

This is a lowercase t.

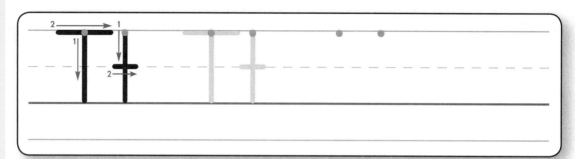

Now trace each **T** and **t** to finish the tongue twister. See if you can say it five times, fast!

Tony eats a tasty taco.

Write the letter **t** to complete the words. Then use each word in an oral sentence to tell about the picture.

__able

__ea

__igers

__ail

# Sight Words

Trace the words. Then draw lines to match the words that are the same.

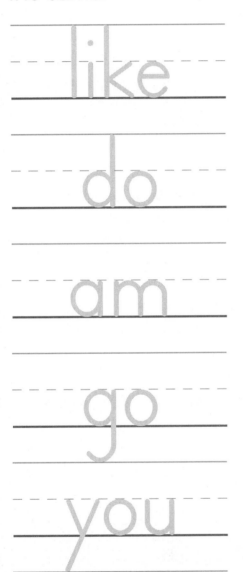

you

am

do

like

go

Write a word to finish this sentence.

.

# Uu

This is an uppercase U.

This is a lowercase u.

Trace and write uppercase **U** and lowercase **u**.

Now trace each **U** and **u** to finish the tongue twister. See if you can say it five times, fast!

Umar wears a uniform.

Follow the steps to draw a unicorn, or draw one from your imagination.

1

2

3

4

What does a unicorn call its father?

*Pop-corn*

Read each word out loud. Draw a circle around each word that has the short u sound. Draw a rectangle around each word that has the long u sound.

umbrella

flute

unicorn

ruler

tub

mug

# Vv

This is an uppercase V.

This is a lowercase v.

Trace and write uppercase V and lowercase v.

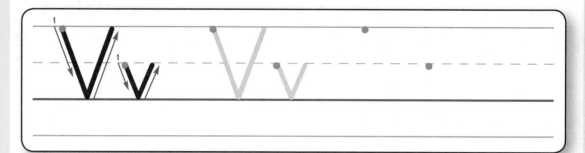

Now trace each V and v to finish the tongue twister. See if you can say it five times, fast!

Vickie drives
a violet van.

What color is each person's safety vest? Read the word above each boater. Then use the key to color in their vests.

vet      vase      violin

**KEY**
vase = blue
vet = yellow
violin = green

# Ww

This is an uppercase W.

This is a lowercase w.

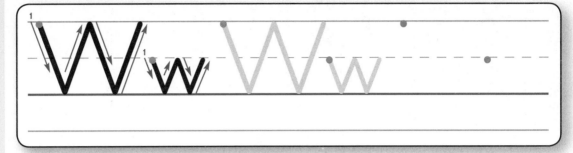

Now trace each **W** and **w** to finish the tongue twister. See if you can say it five times, fast!

Wally swims in water.

Circle the **2** slices of watermelon that match exactly.

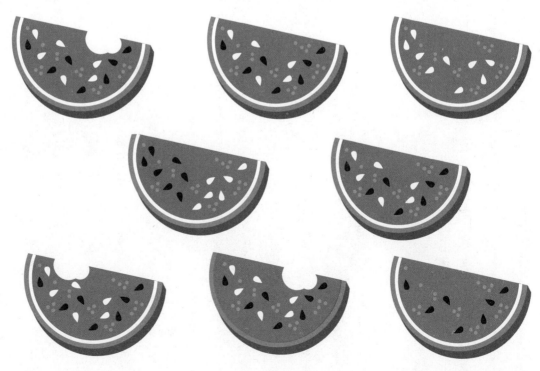

# Xx

This is an uppercase X.

This is a lowercase x.

Trace and write uppercase **X** and lowercase **x**.

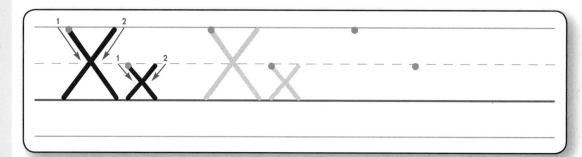

Now trace each **X** and **x** to finish the tongue twister. See if you can say it five times, fast!

This is a T. rex's X-ray.

How many **X**'s can you find in this picture of Xavier Fox?

# Yy

This is an uppercase Y.

This is a lowercase y.

Trace and write uppercase **Y** and lowercase **y**.

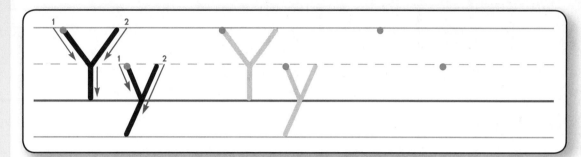

Now trace each **Y** and **y** to finish the tongue twister. See if you can say it five times, fast!

Yanni makes

yummy yogurt

pops.

Trace the lines to see which ball of yarn each cat is using.

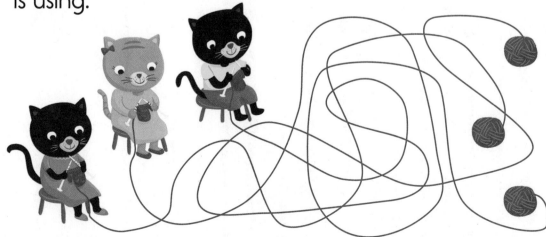

# Zz

This is an uppercase Z.

This is a lowercase z.

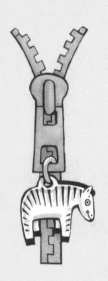

Trace and write uppercase **Z** and lowercase **z**.

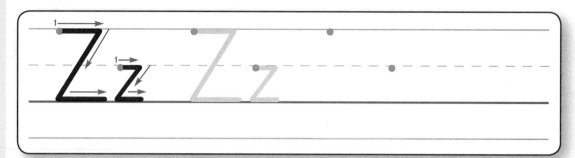

Now trace each **Z** and **z** to finish the tongue twister. See if you can say it five times, fast!

Zander has a zebra zipper.

What a zany zoo! Draw a line from each "creature" to the word with a **z** that might describe it.

buzz

dizzy

jazz

pizza

puzzle

zero

# Color by

Read the words on the crayons. Then
each part of the picture.

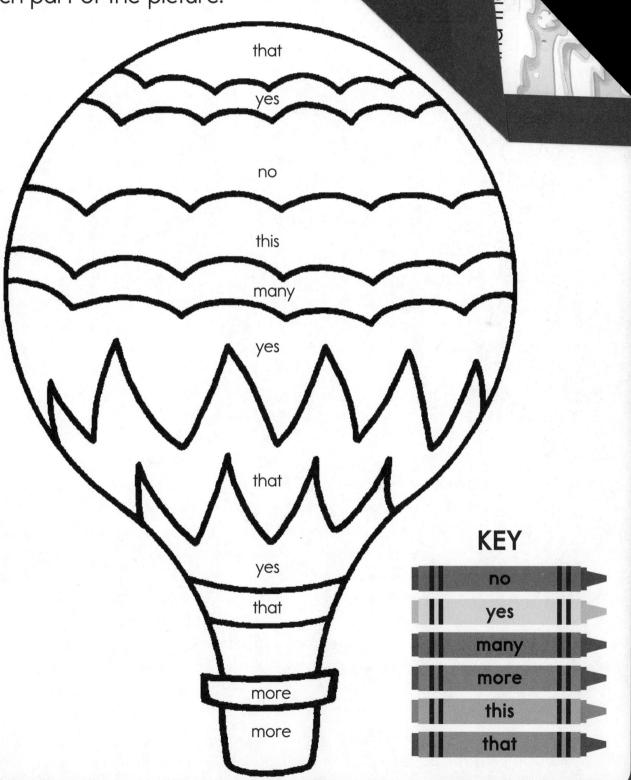

that

yes

no

this

many

yes

that

yes

that

more

more

**KEY**

| no |
| yes |
| many |
| more |
| this |
| that |

# phabet Soup

objects in this Hidden Pictures® puzzle.

pizza

crown

moon

glove

teacup

hat

envelope

football

Read and trace each word. Then write the word.

Mom **made** soup today.

made

Pam and Dan love **her** soup.

her

The noodles **are** letters.

are

Pam makes **words** in her bowl.

words

What letter does Dan **find**?

find

# Uh-Oh!

Circle the words in the story that rhyme.

Read the story, then answer the questions on the next page.

Uh-oh! Look up high.
My balloon is in the sky!

Uh-oh! Watch it go.
It goes over the trees.
Oh, no!

Uh-oh! What's that sound?
*Pop!* My balloon falls down.

It's okay. Look what I see.
Mommy has one more
balloon for me.

What sound does the girl hear?

      ○ *Boom*        ○ *Pop!*        ○ *Zip!*

How does the girl feel at the end of the story?

_____

- - - - - - - - - - - - - - - - - - - - - - - - -

_____

- - - - - - - - - - - - - - - - - - - - - - - - -

_____

Why?

_____

- - - - - - - - - - - - - - - - - - - - - - - - -

_____

- - - - - - - - - - - - - - - - - - - - - - - - -

_____

What does the girl's red balloon go over?

   ○ a zoo        ○ her school        ○ the trees

# Possums in a Pocket

Read the story, then complete the sentences on the next page.

Mama possum has a pocket.
It's safe and warm for her babies to hide.

Six babies come out of the pouch at night.
They climb on her back to take a ride.

They cling on tight to her furry back.
And Mama searches for a berry snack.

Then Mama crawls into her nest as nighttime
fades away.

Her babies snuggle
in the pouch and
rest. They sleep
all through the day.

Do you know of any other animals that have a pouch?

Use a word or phrase from the text to fill in each blank.

Mama possum has a pocket where her

_____

_____ can hide.

Another word for *pocket* is

_____

_____.

The babies climb onto

_____

_____.

The possum babies sleep during the

_____

_____.

# Congratulations!

_____
(your name)

worked hard
and finished the

# Reading
Learning Fun Workbook

KINDERGARTEN

# Answers

## Inside Front Cover

Darcy's helmet is purple.

Ava's shirt is green.

## Page 4
### Aa

## Page 8
### Dd

## Page 9
### It's Rhyme Time!

car — cat
bat — star
cap — tape
ape — map

## Page 10
### Ee

## Page 12
### Ff

## Page 14
### Hh

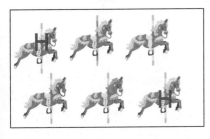

## Page 16
### Ii

## Page 18
### Jj

## Page 20
### Ll

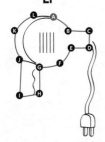

It's a **BLOW-DRYER**.

## Page 23
### Heard Word

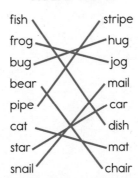

fish — hug
frog — car
bug — mail
bear — dish
pipe — jog
cat — stripe
star — chair
snail — mat

Here are some rhyming pairs we found.
You might have found others.

bone — phone
chew — shoe
crow — sew
dragon — wagon
fat — cat
fruit — suit
letter — sweater
rat — hat
red — bread
snake — cake
troll — hole

# Answers

### Page 26
### Pp

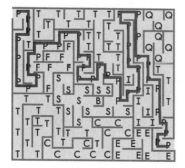

### Page 28
### Rr

### Page 29
### Ss

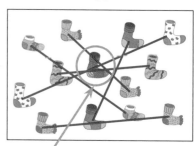

This sock has no match.

### Page 35
### Ww

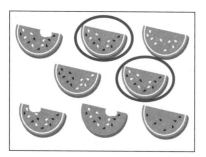

### Page 36
### Xx

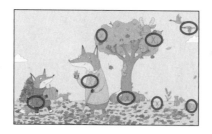

### Page 37
### Yy

### Page 38
### Zz

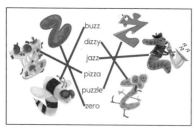

buzz
dizzy
jazz
pizza
puzzle
zero

### Page 40
### Alphabet Soup

### Page 43
### Uh-Oh!

What sound does the girl hear? *Pop!*

How does the girl feel at the end of the story? The girl feels happy.

Why? She feels happy because her mom has a new balloon for her.

What does the girl's red balloon go over? It goes over the trees.

### Page 45
### Possums in a Pocket

Mama possum has a pocket where her **babies** can hide.

Another word for *pocket* is **pouch**.

The babies climb onto **her back**.

The possum babies sleep during the day.

### Inside Back Cover
### Scavenger Hunt

1. Page 38
2. Page 29
3. Page 7
4. Page 10
5. Page 35
6. Page 9